DELIVERANCE FROM FROM TRIANGULAR POWERS

DR.D.K.OLUKOYA

© 2012 A.D. — DELIVERANCE FROM TRIANGULAR POWERS
Dr. D.K. Olukoya

ISBN: 978-978-49174-0-7
A Publication of
TRACTS AND PUBLICATIONS GROUP
MOUNTAIN OF FIRE AND MIRACLES MINISTRIES
13, Olasimbo Street, off Olumo Road,
(By UNILAG Second Gate), Onike, Iwaya.
P.O.Box 2990, Sabo, Yaba, Lagos, Nigeria.
08023308127, 01-7747198, 01-7303485
Website: www.mountainoffire.org
E-mail: mfmhqworldwide@mountainoffire.org

I salute my wonderful wife, Pastor Shade, for her invaluable support in the ministry. I appreciate her unquantifiable support in the book ministry as the Cover designer, Art editor, and Art advisor.

First Edition

TABLE OF CONTENTS

Chapter One

WHAT ARE TRIANGULAR POWERS?

Some people will not prosper until whatever is linking them to the sun, moon and stars is broken to pieces

Most things in life have levels. For example, deliverance has levels, prophets have levels and prayers too, have levels. This explains why some people go for deliverance as many as two hundred times and still do not get delivered. Some people do not understand why the battle is so hard; they do not understand what is happening. There are different kinds of problems and different forms of wickedness. All these things have levels.

PSALM 2

A look at the operations of the dark kingdom shows that demons are really houseboys and messengers compared to the powers mentioned in Psalm 2. When you begin to confront the kind of powers discussed in Psalm 2: 1-3, then you know for sure that you are in for deep deliverance.

Psalm 2: 1-3 says, **"Why do the heathen rage, and the people imagine a vain thing?**

The kings of the earth set themselves, and the rulers take counsel together, against the LORD, and against his anointed, saying, Let us break their bands asunder, and cast away their cords from us."

When you begin to challenge these kinds of powers that are able to take counsel together against the Lord and against His anointed, then you know that you are dealing with very serious issues.

WHAT ARE TRIANGULAR POWERS?

Genesis 1:1 says, **"In the beginning, God created the heavens and the earth."** Genesis is the book of beginnings. The first architect, the first doctor, the first anesthetist, the first murderer, the first thief, etc. are found in the book of Genesis. The first of good and bad things are recorded in the book of Genesis. The first examples of demonic possession and deliverance are also found there.

Genesis 1:1-2 says, **"In the beginning, God created the heaven and the earth. And the earth was without form, and void; and darkness was upon the face of the deep. And the Spirit of God moved upon the face of the waters."**

So right from the beginning of the world, the following conditions existed: "Formlessness, emptiness and darkness. Those are the three conditions that confronted the universe right from the book of Genesis. In the same way, we find that a man's life or a thing could be made shapeless, empty and dark.

Verse 2 says, **"And the Spirit of God moved upon the face of the waters."**

There, as early as in verse 2 of Genesis chapter 1, water was introduced. Up till now, one of the vicious powers we still confront is marine power.

Verse 3: **"And God said, Let there be**

light and there was light."

Anytime God wanted to create something out of nothing, He would say, "Let there be." When He wanted to create man, He did that with His hands. But here He said, "Let there be light" and there was light.

Verses 4-12: **"And God saw the light, that it was good: and God divided the light from the darkness. And God called the light Day, and the darkness he called Night. And the evening and the morning were the first day. And God said, Let there be a firmament in the midst of the waters, and let it divide the waters from the waters. And God made the firmament, and divided the waters which were under the firmament from the waters which were above the firmament: and it was so. And God called the firmament Heaven. And the evening and the morning were the second day. And God said, Let the waters under the heaven be gathered together** unto one place, and let the dry land appear: and it was so. And God called the dry land Earth; and the gathering together of the waters called he Seas: and God saw that it was good. And God said, Let the earth bring forth grass, the herb yielding seed, and the fruit tree yielding fruit after his kind, whose seed is in itself, upon the earth: and it was so. And the earth brought forth grass, and herb yielding seed after his kind, and the tree yielding fruit, whose seed was in itself, after his kind: and God saw that it was good."

It means that plants existed before human beings.

Verses 13-14: "And the evening and the morning were the third day. And God said, Let there be lights in the firmament of the heaven to divide the day from the night; and let them be for signs, and for seasons, and for days, and years."

They were to be for these purposes:

1. Signs.
2. Seasons.
3. Days.
4. Years.

Verses 15-19: **"And let them be for lights in the firmament of the heaven to give light upon the earth: and it was so. And God made two great lights, the greater light to rule the day and the lesser light to rule the night: He made the stars also. And God set them in the firmament of the heaven to give light upon the earth. And to rule over the day and over the night, and to divide the light from the darkness: and God saw that it was good. And the evening and the morning were the fourth day."**

There, we see the triangular powers identified:

- The sun.
- The moon.
- The stars.

These are called the triangular powers, which are located in the heavenlies. The second heaven is the headquarters of darkness and the third heaven is the paradise of God.

What we are looking at is beyond binding demons and casting them out. This is deliverance at the highest level. If somebody is being tormented, harassed and limited by the triangular powers, the "come out" prayer will not help the person because there is nothing inside to cast out. What needs to be done is to break in pieces the controlling powers upon the life of the person. The truth is that as far as there is the sun, the moon and the stars in the sky, some people will not prosper until whatever is linking them to these elements of nature is broken into pieces.

Prayer Points

1. I rule over the powers of darkness in my environment, in the name of Jesus.
2. I chase every demon that threatens my life back to it own kind, in the name of Jesus.
3. I halt every satanic activity against my progress, in the name of Jesus.
4. O God, strengthen me by the Holy Spirit, in the name of Jesus.
5. O Lord, help me to grow stronger in my inner man, in the name of Jesus.
6. I reject the valley of failure and defeat, in the name of Jesus.
7. I invade the territory of the enemy and possess my possessions, in the name of Jesus.

Chapter Two

SOURCES OF THE POWER OF WICKED MEN

Wicked men who hang their powers in the heavenlies are the kind of men you do not fight in a hurry.

Wicked men derive their powers from six sources:

1. The waters.
2. The earth.
3. Familiar spirits.
4. Witchcraft spirits.
5. The elements (fire, water, wind, earth).
6. Triangular powers in the heavenlies.

The most wicked men are those who are able to control the triangular powers. When such men are after a person's life, you know that it is a serious matter. The Psalmist who is an expert in the school of warfare says, "The sun will not smite me by day nor the moon at night," meaning that both the sun and moon have power to smite. Pestilence of the night and destruction at noonday are controlled by the sun, moon and stars.

PEOPLE AND THEIR STARS

Each person has a star attached to his life. Immediately Jesus was born, some people were able to locate His star in the heavenlies and traced it to where He was born. A person becomes useless if his star is tracked down and held by the wicked. He will not be able to locate his star and will not know where his destiny lies. It can be a terrible thing.

A person whose mind wanders during prayers is being controlled by the triangular powers. When after deliverance upon deliverance, a person goes to bed and all the forces come rushing back at night, it is a sign that the triangular powers are at work. If the problems of such a person have been programmed into the moon, there is no way the deliverance of the afternoon will help him because when the moon comes out at night, the programme would be referred to and it starts all over again.

This is why God asked Job: **"Hast thou commanded the morning since thy days; and caused the dayspring to know its** place, that it might take hold of the ends of the earth, that the wicked might be shaken out of it?" (Job 38:12-13).

When a person is always at the lowest step of the ladder, for example, in a class of 40, he would be the 40th person and when the class increases by two persons, he would become number 42, it means that the triangular powers are in charge of his case. As far as the sun remains, he will continue to fail.

Sexual immorality and all kinds of atrocities have greater tendency to increase when there is full moon. When there is full moon, all kinds of evil spiritual activities begin to take place. In some places, terrible witches do not operate until there is full moon, then problem starts. Hence, anywhere you see the picture of the full moon as a symbol, know that you are looking at serious witchcraft in the heavenlies.

A person who has no friend at all and cannot point to anybody that loves him or her and even the husband or wife is a danger to him or her, has triangular powers at work in his or her life. A person who comes for deliverance and all the prayer points have no effect on him or her, has triangular powers in charge of his or her case.

Our forefathers understood the triangular powers more than we do. They knew what they were doing but the modern day man is still so confused, he does not know his left from his right and so, there is trouble for him.

Wicked men, who hang their powers in the heavenlies are the kind of men you do not fight in a hurry. They know what they are doing. They know that as far as the heaven is above men, whoever controls the heavenlies controls the earth. Therefore, a person who would sit down somewhere and his mind is thousands of miles away, cannot concentrate, even to read his Bible or pray is a problem, is being controlled by triangular powers. If you see a person who is praying and fasting so hard, yet the enemy's attack increases even as he is losing weight in the process, know straight away that it is no longer demons that are in charge of the person's problems but powers higher than them.

The kind of powers we read about in Psalm 2 are not the kind you just bind and cast out. If you bind and cast them out, they will be laughing at you and wondering what you know about deliverance. These are the top-ranking angels who were once with God at the beginning. They were the kind of angels who confronted those taking the body of Moses away and they contended for his body until Angel Michael had to say, "The Lord rebuke thee" (Jude 1:9). It was then the body of Moses was released. They were the kind of powers that stood as the Prince of Persia which disturbed the prayer of Daniel for twenty-one days until reinforcement was sent. These are not the kind of powers you bind and cast out in deliverance. No, you will have to raise the level of your battle.

Judges 5:19-20 says, **"The kings came and fought, then fought the kings of Canaan in Taanach by the waters of Megiddo; they took no gain of money. They fought from heaven; the stars in their courses fought against Sisera."**

So, the stars can fight. There are many people who come for deliverance and say that the sun or the moon is pursuing them. These elements enter right into their bodies.

When Joseph started talking about his dream, he said, "I saw stars bowing down." Immediately, his brothers understood it. They knew that the stars which the boy was referring to, represented their destiny. Their stars bowing down to Joseph's own means that the star of a person can be made to bow down, and the brothers did not like what he was saying.

The enemy can always make the star of a

person to bow down and anywhere the person is, no matter how intelligent, superior or knowledgeable he may be, he will not prosper; he will be below people that he is better than.

When a deliverance candidate comes before you and you try your normal deliverance prayers and they do not work or you give the person prayer points, and there is still no way rather the person says the attack is increasing, you should immediately suspect that triangular powers are at work. Also, you must learn how to disconnect people from triangular powers. You must know also that the personal star of a person can be located and cast down.

There are many professors who are selling chicken now. There are many doctors who have become poultry farmers. There are many people with high-sounding degrees that are now in psychiatric hospitals. There are many people who are supposed to be shining stars but they are being trodden underfoot. The enemy has located their stars and has cast them down. These are very serious matters as they go beyond the normal deliverance.

I want you to know that satan is struggling so hard to prevent Christians from understanding the triangular powers. That is why you will hardly find a church where you are taught about the sun, the moon and the stars. He will not allow them to teach such things rather they would teach people things like holiness, love, fear of God, etc. The enemy does not have problems with people knowing about the things that will get them to heaven. But before people get to heaven, they must survive on earth. A person does not have to go to heaven Lazarus-style. Abraham enjoyed himself and went to heaven. Lazarus suffered and also went to heaven. So, why not go to heaven the Abraham style?

THE RELIGION OF THE BONDWOMAN

The bondwoman's religion is so strong

because it is connected with the sun, the moon and the stars. Anytime, people of this religion wake up in the morning, they chant incantations and enchantments to serve the triangular powers. Unfortunately, the triangular powers are neutral powers. They operate on first come, first serve basis. So, what you programme into them is what they will do, unless you have a higher power or higher anointing like Moses. Moses spoke to the earth and the magicians of Egypt did so too. But after some time, both Moses and the magicians spoke again to the earth but the earth did not listen to the instructions of the magicians any longer. You can command the triangular powers to reject the instructions of your enemy by praying like this: "Thou triangular powers, reject the instructions of my enemies, in the name of Jesus."

The prophecy about Ishmael said that His hand shall be upon every man, and every man's hand shall be upon him. He shall be a wild man; a wild man who will not agree but must fight everyone (Genesis 16:12). Unfortunately, this wild man whose hands shall be upon every man and every man's hands shall be upon him understands the heavenlies while many Christians do not. His own people understand the greatest source of power but many Christians do not.

As far as you still find people waking up early in the morning to make enchantments while Christians are still busy snoring, deliverance from these powers will be difficult. Until Christians sit up and before the children of the bondwoman begin their early morning cry, they are already saying, "Father, in the name of Jesus" then there would be progress.

Christians find it difficult to control them because they wake up earlier than most Christians. They pour their enchantments into the sky before a lot of Christians wake up to take control of the day. It is even sad to know that there are some Christians who fall asleep while reading their Bibles in the morning. Christians must understand that dealing with this religion of greater abomination requires hard work.

Prayer Points

1. O God, contend with those who contend with me, in the name of Jesus.
2. Every anti-testimony altar erected against me, be dismantled by fire, in the name of Jesus.
3. Anything that does not work heavenly programmes in my life, die, in the name of Jesus.
4 I withdraw satan's mandate against my destiny, in the name of Jesus.
5. Blood of Jesus, recover my stolen birthright, in the name of Jesus.
6. O Lord, kill every internal destiny killer in my life, in the name of Jesus.
7. Every agenda of the bondwoman and her baby against my life, family, ministry and calling, scatter, in the name of Jesus.

Chapter Three

TRIANGULAR POWERS AND WITCHCRAFT

Nobody can kill men and women who know how to deal with triangular powers

ASTRAL TRAVEL

Sometimes, wicked people go on astral travels. It is a process whereby their spirits are taken out on a journey. Astral travel is undertaken to look closely at the heavenlies and send enchantments and incantations on the star of a person. This type of situation cannot be solved by normal deliverance prayers.

Triangular powers are the ones that empower witches and wizards. Witchcraft is more than blood-sucking. It has to do with the sun, the moon and the stars. That is where they get their powers from. That is why an African witch is that person that can get her spirit out of her body and bring it back again. It is known as astral travel. It is not everybody that can perform that feat. When most people sleep that is it, but there are many people, who when they sleep, another world begins for them. They will get out of their physical bodies and begin to do havoc.

Some of what some women call spirit husbands are not spirit husbands but spirit of men who like them but know that physically, they will never agree to follow them. So, they wait for them to sleep and transfer their spirits out of their bodies to join them at night.

I know a certain woman who went to the hospital for medical treatment. She was 60 years old and the doctor she met there was 30 years old. The doctor proposed to have a sexual relationship with her and she refused. The doctor said, "Okay, you think you are powerful. I will see you tonight." And by that night, she said that something appeared to her like a crocodile with a male organ as big as a man's hand and almost finished her up. When she woke up, she was bleeding. By the time she went back to the hospital, the same doctor said, "I told you, I will come for a woman of sixty." So, he took his spirit out of his physical body to go and do evil at night.

She had to be prayed for violently before she recovered. She went to the hospital with one problem and came back with another. This kind of people derive their power from the triangular sources. Any ministry that does not understand deliverance will soon collapse.

STARS CAN SPEAK

Another thing you need to know is that stars have mouth. Satanic prophets consult stars to pick up information about people. If they want to know about a person, they will call the person's star and find out.

They are in three categories:

Those who use water.

Those who use mirror.

Those who use crystal balls.

Some, who are very poor use water. They call the person's face or star into the water and command the star to speak and the star would say, "I belong to this person. I am the star of his life. I am supposed to be in America by now. I am supposed to have built so many houses. I am the breadwinner of this family. I am supposed to be this or that. This is what the Almighty has programmed into me."

Stars speak to herbalists. The herbalists would say, "Okay you are supposed to be here but you have not got there yet." Then they take steps to block the person. Many people have been blocked since they were babies. Some people, who have been saying, "I don't know, I have been praying but nothing seems to be changing," should thank God that they are even still living. They would have been dead but the power of God preserved them.

The poor satanic prophets use water. Immediately you enter a place and see water stored in various pots, not because of water shortage, know that you are dealing with somebody who consults stars.

There are also those who make use of the mirror. If you enter into the bedroom of someone and find a particular mirror covered with cloth, aside from a normal mirror which he has, know that he is a consulter of the stars. So, whenever he wants to consult them, he would open the mirror and call up a person's star in that mirror and the star will tell him all the secrets.

The rich ones amongst the satanic agents use crystal balls. When a person's star is called from the crystal ball, his destiny, who he is, what he is attaining, whether he is fulfilling his destiny or not, and every other information about him would be known. Right there, they can cut the person off, and sniff out his star. When a person is cut off like that and he goes to the deliverance ground and begins to bind every foundational or ancestral bondage and to cast out whatever, he would not make progress because the trouble is that his star has been cast out, removed, caged, diverted or buried. So, he needs to pray a resurrection prayer. It is all part of deliverance too but another kind of deliverance.

Sometime ago, a woman's husband was pushing leaves into her hand in the dark. By the time she switched on the light, she pushed away the leaves and ran out. But her husband followed and begged her not to tell anyone. She insisted on knowing the reason he did that before closing her mouth. The man told her that she had twenty-one shining stars and he had only two according to where he went to consult. He told her that he was told that even the two stars he had were already taken away by his grandmother when he was growing up leaving him with none. And that if he was going to prosper at all, she would have to lose all her stars to him. So, he wanted to withdraw her stars because as long as she had them, she would be the husband and he, the wife. The man planned a strategy to remove her stars but it was not possible.

These people check the stars in the water,

through the mirror and crystal balls. They want every information they can get before they fire their arrows.

You must understand your environment and be able to control it. Nobody can kill men and women who know how to deal with triangular powers. No witch can kill them unless the witch wants to die because by the time they begin to programme words into the sun, moon and stars, the witch will be in trouble.

LIGHT MANIPULATION

One of the most important factors of life is light. Without light, nobody can do anything; the entire place will be in darkness. The enemy can manipulate the light that shines upon people. Knowing that without light, there is no existence, they manipulate the kind of light that will shine upon a person. The enemy can make the light of disgrace to shine upon a person or prevent the correct light from shining upon him. That is, the person will never be in a place where he will have opportunity. He will always be at a dead end, where the road is closed. When you see such a case, know that triangular powers are at work.

The enemy can conjure a star, give the star the name of somebody and cast it down. All of a sudden, the person will fall from grace to grass. It is very sad.

The kingdom of darkness is a dangerous place. There is always a fight for survival, positions and all kinds of things. All kinds of evil go on there. There are some spirits that are so strong in the demonic realm that sometimes, they disobey even the devil. They are able to do that because while they were in heaven together, their ranks were not far apart before they fell together. If they are told to break one hand, they can break three. This is because they are disobedient.

Loss of property can be programmed into

the stars. Victims just notice that they are losing their property little by little, and they know that they are not possessed and by the grace of God, they are doing their best but they are losing their property.

Triangular powers are responsible for people's inability to practise holiness, especially men of God. We must learn to take our warfare to the sun, moon and stars; the triangular powers.

THE SUN

The sun is 93 million miles away. Despite that distance, the heat can be felt on earth. The sun represents open aggressive enemies. That is, they are not hidden.

When a certain sister got married, her mother-in-law came to her and said, "Well. I just came to inform you that I am the first wife and you are number two. If you keep to that formula, there will be no problem." The sister said, "I reject it, in Jesus' name," and the mother-in-law said, "You are rejecting it, okay." To her amazement, the first day the mother-in-law came visiting, her husband drove her out of their bedroom. Her mother-in- law slept on the same bed with her husband. The sister became stubborn and joined them on the bed. So, the three of them slept on the same bed. When you see such strange things happening, know that triangular powers are in charge. That mother-in-law was an open unashamed enemy.

Also, I have seen a situation where a strange woman followed a sister into her matrimonial home and said, "Excuse me, Madam, I want to have your husband for some time." And the man carried his briefcase and followed her. When his wife called him back, he did not answer. He went away with the strange woman - triangular powers.

Men and women who operate in that realm

are very proud because they know that they can do and undo people. They would have the weakest argument and point and would be the ones shouting the loudest.

THE MOON

The moon is a subtle and clever enemy. It is very nice on the surface, cool, calm and gentle but very dangerous. If you face that kind of enemy, you need to pray some prayers.

Prayer Points

1. I nullify every satanic decree and desire against my life by the power in the blood of Jesus, in the name of Jesus.
2. Every witchcraft kitchen preparing evil food for me, catch fire, in the name of Jesus.
3. Every witchcraft tree caging the labour of my hands, catch fire, in the name of Jesus.
4. Every dragon power swallowing my prayers, I command your stomach to burst into flames, in the name of Jesus.
5. Every witchcraft horn raised against me, scatter, in the name of Jesus.
6. Every altar erected against me by day, be dismantled, in the name of Jesus.
7. Every altar erected against me by night, be dismantled, in the name of Jesus.

Chapter Four

TRIANGULAR POWERS AND CHARMS

When your words do not carry weight in heaven or on earth, you are watching the serpent of the magician

WHAT IS A CHARM?

1. A charm is an inanimate object to which demonic powers have been attached to carry out evil assignments. There is nothing bad spirits cannot attach to. There is a limit to what you can bind, cast out and sanctify. If somebody digs up an idol from the ground and does not know it is an idol, and unconsciously makes jewelry out of it, anyone that puts it on becomes a demon carrier. There is no prayer you can pray to take the idol away. The best thing is to throw it away. When a demon is tied to an object, it is called a charm.

2. A charm is an object of the power of darkness programmed to bewitch.

3. It is an object used for evil summon.

4. It is a small station for enchantment and spell.

5. It is a magical object to manipulate, dominate and control.

6. It is an object backed up by idol powers.

7. It is an object fashioned to fire satanic arrows. That is why someone can put a demonic broom at the door of a family house and there would be disharmony among the members of that household.

8. It is a prescribed action or formula backed up with satanic anointing.

Charms can be used against animals, human beings, plants and even marriages or to transfer people's virtues. In the book of Exodus, you will find that in Pharaoh's court, the magicians, who had occult powers produced more serpents than Moses. But the Lord does not work with numbers. A single serpent of Moses swallowed all their serpents. So, they had their own powers, no doubt, and with their powers, they produced their own serpents. If you stand watching the serpents of the magicians without taking action, they will bite you and you will die. So, you have to take action.

WHAT IN PRACTICAL SPIRITUAL TERMS DOES IT MEAN TO WATCH THE SERPENT OF THE MAGICIAN?

If you have ever been served food in your dream and you could not resist it, you are watching the serpent of the magician.

If you cannot resist spirit spouses when they come to you in the dream; they succeed in messing you up, you are watching the serpent. If in your dream, some people were running after you with all kinds of weapons and when they used them against you, they worked, you are watching the serpent. Inability to resist spiritual arrows indicates that you are watching the serpent of the magician.

If you are a victim, it is time for you to cry out in anger that the fire of God should burst forth in your life. It is time for you to pray that God should make you hot coals of fire, too hot for the enemy to move close to. It is time to pray to receive the fire that no evil power can resist. Whatsoever affects your spiritual life negatively and leaves you helpless and you just become a spectator is a killer. You must deal with it.

MARKS OF THOSE WHO ARE WATCHING THE SERPENTS OF THE MAGICIANS

1. Inability to resist spiritual arrows.
2. Inability to come against dream attackers.
3. Weakness in the face of spiritual attacks.
4. Lack of knowledge of the operation of evil powers.
5. Inability to fight and win. When you are tired of evil attacks and drop your prayers because anytime you pray, you will be attacked, you are watching the serpent of the magician.
6. Inability to fight back.
7. Lack of knowledge of the identity of the

serpent.

8. When the enemy is using your body to test new spiritual weapons, you are watching the serpent of the magician.

9. When you watch dangerous and strange sights, you are watching the serpent of the magician.

10. Anytime the weapons of the enemy prosper in a person's life or the enemy disarms a person, the person is watching the serpent of the magician.

11. When you are completely ignorant of the kind of warfare that you are fighting, you are watching the serpent of the magician.

12. When your words do not carry weight in heaven or on earth, you are watching the serpent of the magician.

That is why you need to cry out and declare that the lion of your life must roar, and fear must enter into the camp of your enemies, and the fear must cause a scattering.

WHY DO PEOPLE BECOME SPECTATORS AT THE ARENA OF THE SERPENTS OF THE MAGICIANS?

1. Ignorance.

2. Worldliness: Many sisters are becoming more and more worldly. They wear transparent clothes even to the church. Some wear the kind of blouses that expose their chests. Worldliness makes the serpents to rage. Some threw away their giant earrings and replaced them with tiny ones. It is worldliness. If God wanted you to put on earrings, He would have punched your ears from your mother's womb. If God wanted men and women to be smoking cigarettes, He would have put chimneys on their heads from the womb. So, God knows what He is doing. He is a God of perfection but many Christians do not understand what they are doing. Occultists would design jewelry and believers who are supposed to have knowledge would buy and put it on. And after they have put it on, they begin to sing, "Spirit husband, go back to your sender, go back to your sender." Who is the sender? The spirit husband will not go because his material is on their bodies.

Wearing of earrings started with slavery. An earring in one ear indicated that the wearer belonged to one slave master. Two meant two slave masters, you served one in the morning; and the other in the evening. When slavery eased out, the slaves who were ashamed in the market place or wherever they were, began to use something to block those holes. So, Christians who use these things are copying slavery.

3. **Lack of internal peace:** Your peace of mind is your proof of victory. Jesus commanded peace during the storm and there was peace. That was the evidence of His authority. When the powers of darkness did their worst with Jesus at the parlour of Pilate, He was cool, calm and collected. If you do not have peace in your life, you have war and if you have victory, you have peace. That is why the Bible says, "The God of peace shall bruise satan under your feet shortly (Romans 16:20).

4. Unbelief: This prevents a person from resting in God.

5. Lack of recognition of your authority in Christ.

6. Attack by forces of evil renewal: This is talking about the powers that wake up evil things that are already dead.

7. Laziness: Lazy people do not begin things.

Sometimes, they will agree to do a thing only to put it off. Little by little, they surrender until it becomes total defeat. Lazy people never get going. Procrastination is the child of laziness. People who never develop a sense of urgency about life drift from one action to another. Some people are too lazy to pray, read the Bible and witness. They do not face what they are supposed to face. They do not contribute much to other people's lives. That is why it is a disaster in marriage when one partner is lazy. The whole family may live in poverty because one party is too lazy.

The lazy man is always restless. He wants more but does not want to put in more. The lazy man is a useless person because he will not do what he is supposed to do. If you are lazy, God cannot use you in His plan. If you are lazy, you will continue to be a servant to others all your life. A lazy man is an unbeliever. He has no faith. He would say, "Ah, this is wonderful but I won't be able to do it." A lazy person would be poor. So, spiritual laziness is the number one factor that turns people to spectators in the arena of the battle of the serpent.

When a person is spiritually lazy, he would have deep hatred for anything that would make him sit down and read the Bible or pray. He would have deep hatred for anything that would move his spiritual life forward. When a lazy man begins a spiritual exercise, all of a sudden, other things that he has left undone will begin to surface and call for his attention. When a lazy man engages in a spiritual exercise, whether Bible study or prayer, something inside him would ask him to stop. The lazy man turns about on his bed but does not get out of it. And eventually, when he is out of that bed, he would wish to go back there. The lazy man would sleep at 10.00pm and still feel too lazy to get up at 7.00am. He would sleep half the day and waste the major part of the time watching television. He is too lazy to nourish even his own spiritual life.

Spiritual laziness is the bane of the modern man. All forms of spiritual dryness can be blamed on laziness. Sometimes, poor attendance of church services is due to laziness. This is why you need to pray that the Lord should deliver you from anything that would sit you down in the arena of the battle of the serpents and make you a mere spectator.

If you keep watching the serpent, a time would come when the serpent would move to where you are and bite you.

You need to come to terms with yourself, confront your laziness and weakness. Pray that your zeal and fire should come to a boiling point. When you are burning hot with the fire of God, no demon can come near you.

Prayer Points

1. My life, explode by fire, in the name of Jesus.
2. My life, burst forth, in the name of Jesus.
3. Thou suppressing power, die, in the name of Jesus.
4. O serpent of God, arise and kill the serpent of my father's house, in the name of Jesus.
5. My life, roar like a lion and kill your problems, in the name of Jesus.
6. Every good thing that has passed me by, come back and locate me, in the name of Jesus.
7. My spirit man, be charged with the fire of God that no enemy can touch, in the name of Jesus.

Chapter Five

HOW
TO
HANDLE
CHARMS

The presence of God is not the noisy manifestation of demonic activities

HOW TO HANDLE CHARMS

If you have not yet surrendered your life to Jesus, then you cannot deal with the serpent of the magician disturbing your destiny and you cannot deal with charms and charmers.

According to Acts 19, the final resting place for charms and fetishes is fire. Paul collected and burnt them to ashes.

You can pray deprogramming prayers on them. You can say:

➢I dismantle your demons, in the name of Jesus.

➢I command your demons not to have access, in the name of Jesus.

➢I cancel your assignments, in the name of Jesus.

However, if you want to be much more aggressive, you can ask the triangular powers to carry the warfare back to their senders.

Christians are supposed to be very dangerous people but sometimes, they do not use the power available to them. The reason for this is that some of them are still struggling with fornication, lying, etc.

Unfortunately, some ministers believe that they are the best in the world because when they pray for some people, they begin to manifest. They consider it as great not knowing that most times, the manifestations are just entertainment by these powers to make the heads of the ministers to swell and they will think that they are powerful. The day they fire at them, they will not be able to stand.

A lot of times, great deliverance takes place without anybody uttering one word. The presence of God is not the noisy manifestation of demonic activities. The presence of God is like the kind of thing Elijah saw. Elijah was not moved by the noise, earthquake and thunder. But when there was the still small voice, he came out and confirmed the presence of God (1 Kings 19).

A great deliverance can take place in a person's life with just a shed of tears. Most deliverance ministers do not believe that there is deliverance until the entire place is scattered. When the whole place is upside down, they believe they are doing well whereas by the time the deliverance candidates go home, they find that there has been no deliverance. Some people even believe now that if you do not make some whistling sounds and people fall down, you do not have the power of God. What is important is to know the essential things to do.

It is very important for you to know that triangular powers are very tricky so, you must rely on the Holy Spirit for instructions.

Prayer Points

1. You lion of my life, roar by fire, pursue your pursuers, in the name of Jesus.
2. Wall of protection around every charm targeted against me, die, in the name of Jesus.
3. The fetish working against my destiny, die, in the name of Jesus.
4. Every charm programmed against my life, backfire, in the name of Jesus.
5. Every satanic animal charmed against my body, swallow your owner, in the name of Jesus.
6. My prayer arrow, arise and shoot down any satanic bird flying against me, in the name of Jesus.
7. Every charmer of my father's house, what are you waiting for? Die, in the name of Jesus.

8. Every charm fashioned against my finances, I render you impotent, in the name of Jesus.

9. Every environmental charm and charmer, scatter, in the name of Jesus.

10. Every satanic ammunition by envious enemies, backfire, in the name of Jesus.

11. Every power planning to use charms against me, die, in the name of Jesus.

Chapter Six

PRAYERS OF DELIVERANCE FROM TRIANGULAR POWERS

Prayer Points

1. I disconnect my life from the evil control of triangular powers, in Jesus' name.
2. Every arrow from the sun, moon and stars, release me and locate your owner, in the name of Jesus.
3. Let the stars fight for me and not against me, in the name of Jesus.
4. I command the triangular powers to go into war for me, in the name of Jesus.
5. O heavens, refuse to carry warfare into my life, in the name of Jesus.
6. Every evil thing programmed into my family line from the stars, be cancelled, in the name of Jesus.
7. Every evil star that followed my parents, my life is not your candidate, in the name of Jesus.
8. O sun, vomit bewitchment upon your sender, in the name of Jesus.
9. Anything in my life that will prevent the

heavenlies from fighting for me, come out, in the name of Jesus.

10. Every enchantment and ordinance of satanists in the heavenlies against me, backfire, in the name of Jesus.

11. Blood of Jesus, wipe away every evil handwriting that is in the heavenlies against me, in name of Jesus.

12. The sun shall not smite me by day nor the moon by night, in the name of Jesus.

13. Mirror and crystal ball of darkness, break, in the name of Jesus.

14. Every bewitchment of my star, die, in the name of Jesus.

15. Any power that wants the star of my destiny to bow, die, in the name of Jesus.

16. The star of my destiny shall not bow, in the name of Jesus.

17. O voice of my star, disgrace my attackers, in the name of Jesus.

18. Every power calling my star into the water, burn to ashes, in the name of Jesus.
19. I decree that my star will not be called into the water, in the name of Jesus.
20. Every evil light shining upon my destiny, die, in the name of Jesus.
21. O Lord, raise an adversary against the enemies of my destiny, in the name of Jesus.

OTHER BOOKS BY DR.D.K.OLUKOYA

1. 20 Marching Order To Fulfill Your Destiny
2. 30 Things The Anointing Can Do For You
3. 30 Poverty-Destroying Keys
4. 30 Prophetic Arrows From Heaven
5. A-Z Of Complete Deliverance
6. Abraham's Children In Bondage
7. Basic Prayer Patterns
8. Battle Against the Wasters
9. Be Prepared
10. Becoming Extraordinary Among The Ordinary
11. Bewitchment Must Die
12. Biblical Principles Of Dream Interpretation
13. Biblical Principles Of Long Life
14. Born Great, But Tied Down
15. Born To Overcome
16. Breaking Bad Habits
17. Breakthrough Prayers For Business Professionals
18. Bringing Down The Power Of God
19. Brokenness
20. Can God Trust You?
21. Can God?
22. Charge Your Battery
23. Command The Morning
24. Connecting To The God Of Breakthroughs
25. Consecration Commitment & Loyalty
26. Contending For The Kingdom
27. Criminals In The House Of God

Made in United States
Orlando, FL
23 June 2023

34465776R00046